The Collected Poems of Layton Elliott

By Layton Elliott

PublishAmerica
Baltimore

© 2005 by Layton Elliott.
All rights reserved. No part of this book may be reproduced, stored in a retrieval system or transmitted in any form or by any means without the prior written permission of the publishers, except by a reviewer who may quote brief passages in a review to be printed in a newspaper, magazine or journal.

First printing

ISBN: 1-4137-9451-3
PUBLISHED BY PUBLISHAMERICA, LLLP
www.publishamerica.com
Baltimore

Printed in the United States of America

Dedicated to Pam and Andrea

About Embedded Names:

Some of the sonnets in this book contain embedded names. To find these names you must take the first letter of the first line, the second letter of the second line, the third letter of the third line, etc. Some of the embedded names take all fourteen lines, while others only use a portion of the lines available.

Good hunting!

Part One
Life

Forever in Darkness

Forever in darkness I go my way
Year after year, day after day
Over and above, far and away
In the Valley of the Shadow I fall and I pray
But truth is fleeting and it will not stay.

It occurred to me at some point in my life that many truths do not seem to be absolute, but relative, and are only true from your frame of reference.

Mighty Is the Ocean

Mighty is the ocean
Calling out to me;
But I'm afraid to go,
Afraid to set to sea.

Quiet is the harbor
Glowing in the night;
Beckoning me back again
To the safety of the light.

But it was all an illusion
To lure us within its walls,
For the sea goes on forever
Through the continental halls.

I saw a special (on the Discovery Channel, I think) and they talked about these deep trenches in the oceans called the continental halls.

The Path

See if the rain will ever stop the day
Or darkness ever come without the night;
Or heroes ever quit without a fight,
Or June would come before the month of May.
To challenge all we hold to be the truth,
To question all authority we know;
To share your evening meal with a foe
And keep him safe and dry beneath your roof;
For what are we to do if all is done,
And where are we to go if we are there;
And what is work to us if it's not fun?
An obstacle that's much too large to bear?
For life is not the reaching of your goal,
But rather this: the path on which you go.

A sonnet! And in my favorite rhyming pattern! I honestly don't remember when or why I wrote this, but the last two lines I tend to live by.

Brenda

It was a long and tedious journey
To where you don't belong,
But for a feeling of security
You've made this place your home.

Partners came and partners went
With promises not kept long;
Or promises not accepted
When they tried to keep you down.

There's a dream on the edge of consciousness
Just out of fingers' reach;
Perhaps it's at the drowning point
Just beyond the beach.

Maybe you could make it
If you estimate the tide,
Allowing for the current
That swept us all aside.

If you mix a little charity
With a dash of faith and hope
You can overcome disparity
With this magic rope.

Tie it firmly around yourself
And swim with all your might
Until you touch your dream
And set all things to right.

I know you can do it, Bren
I see it in your face;
Be anything you want to be,
You can find your place.

Some dreams come and some dreams go
And some, they have no home;
But hold on to that special dream
And never be alone.

I had a friend at work back in the early nineties, and found out that while the rest of us had our heads buried in our work, she had broken up with her husband and gotten a divorce without displaying a single clue to the rest of us! (At least not to me; I can't really speak for everyone.) Based on what I knew about her, I wrote her this poem for her birthday. I would like to think that this helped her on her way to her new husband and a lasting happiness.

Perpetual Trek

I want to go sailing with Captain Kirk
To every cosmic sky;
The silver starships flittering on,
The planets flickering by;

In search of comrades, in search of peace,
The Federation fills my eyes!
Klingon vessels disappear,
Our phasers running dry.

My reactors, now, are an eon old,
My crystal's cracked and cries;
Place me now in Vulcan soil,
Transport me to the skies!

To be a soldier in sailor garb,
A pilot of *Enterprise*
"First Officer Spock, to the bridge—
Stand by your captain's side."

Dr. McCoy, is that you, then?
Heal me quickly, Bones!
Old age is catching up with me,
Life's river's running home.

"You heartless, tin-plated son-of-a-computer,"
McCoy would say again,
"If you weren't so sick, you'd heal yourself."
Physician, do the same.

I've outlived you, *Starship Enterprise*,
McCoy and Captain Kirk;
I've seen the universal plan
Of ages put to work.

Ohura, Chekov, Sulu, Scot,
The odds that we defied!
"First Officer Spock, to the bridge—
Stand by your captain's side."

I wrote this when I was nineteen, I think—before they killed Spock off in a movie, then brought him back to life in the next; and well before we found him still living and working in the Next Generation. I always thought that Leonard Nimoy could make a lot of money doing a reading with Trek theme music playing in the background.

Dogtown and the Z-Boys

Dogtown's so tame since the Z-Boys grew up;
The old surf shop is gone and the boards are all hung up;
Water in the pools where skaters used to fly;
Dogtown's not the same since the Z-Team said goodbye.

Most left for money,
Some left for drugs;
Some left for a family,
Others can't be found.

Goodbye, Z-Boys,
No more hanging berts
In empty swimming pools;
The sirens and the hurt.

Long-haired athletes with an artistic bent
Broken homes, broken hearts
But no one broke their necks

Outcast from society,
Stealing for a meal;
Building boards from scraps
With the outlaw appeal.

True American heroes
Each and every one
They gave it all they had;
All they had and then plus one!

This poem was written after watching (twice) the documentary of the same name (well before the movie Lords of Dogtown *came out). I have purposely written the poem with different rhythms, rhyming patterns and styles, reflecting the Z-Boys' creativity and freedom of expression.*

Ambition

My life seems to circle around
The movement in the trees
When the clouds part for a little while
And the sun affects the breeze
I want to lie back on the hill
And watch the river flow
But my ambition for a position
In life won't let me go.

This was actually the ending of a longer poem written when I was a teenager; this is the only part I found salvageable.

Solitary Soul

What a strange sensation,
This empty kind of pain;
The feeling of rejection
That cannot be explained.

The doctors, the drugs,
The tears and the fear,
The pressure ever forming;
Ever venting new frontiers.

First there was the throbbing—
Explosions in my head!
Then there was the wheezing
That brought me near to dead;

And now at last I'm crying,
Losing all control;
Locking up my thoughts,
Throwing them in the hole.

A thousand tiny stars
Twinkle in the night
While a solitary soul
Bids the world goodnight.

Severe depression—I fought my way back.

The Butterfly

As I lay in bed, prepared to die,
I thought myself a butterfly;
Wrapped in my sheet, a fitting cocoon,
My visions developed till far past noon.

Through the blackness dark, the visions came;
Bright colors flashing in my brain;
Then the wall began to fall,
Revealing nothing, revealing all!

I saw quite clearly, tho' my eyes were closed,
People and places I did not know—
Perhaps an old man rocking in a chair
Or children playing without a care.

I saw a road, dark and long—
Lifeless trees, waving on;
The blackened hills along the road
Gave no hope, and all was cold.

And when I came back to life again
I got off the road that I began
And tried to correct where I'd gone wrong
And find the road that leads me home.

I do tend to have visions occasionally; whether they actually mean something other than being overly tired, I do not know.

The Falling Star

I saw a star fall through the sky;
I looked to God and asked him why
With all the stars that shine so bright
Should one small star give off such light
And then just fade to endless night?

He just looked back with a million eyes
That twinkled over the unheard cries
Of the untold countless questions said,
Of all generations, living and dead,
In many books writ, yet unread;

And as the night fell to day
And the stars were hid to come what may;
And the sleeping rose to live their life—
Father, daughter, son and wife;
Come then, joy, and come then, strife.

Give to us our daily bread—
Some are full, some unfed;
Some will suffer for all we've lost,
Some will never pay the cost;
The simple choice of the coin we tossed.

My darling Pamela, who has gone through some dark times.

Feather on the Water

There was a feather on the water
And it moved along with ease
Relying on the power
Of the gentle breeze

I want to be that feather
And travel windward ho
No decisions to be made
Just travel with the flow.

Just a little peace.

Someone Else to Care

Please don't shut me out again;
I can bear no more.
If I knew what you were dealing with
I could help, I'm sure.

Just give me half a chance
And I will be right there;
Sometimes all a person needs
Is someone else to care.

It doesn't matter what you've done,
I see the real you;
Though years of pain weigh upon your brow
Your soul comes shining through.

For Pamela.

Tweakers

Hide your lawnmower, lock your bike
The Tweakers all are out tonight
Like locusts in your neighborhood
They take everything left in sight

Have you seen a Tweaker?
It's an ugly thing
Holes all over its yellow face
With rotten teeth for fangs

You can't talk sense to a Tweaker
Half its brain is fried
They want more money to buy more meth
With total lack of pride

You see the Tweakers come out at night
And storm the neighborhood
Anything that they can carry off
Is fenced as stolen goods

You can catch a Tweaker while it sleeps
That's your very best chance
They sleep for 3 or 4 days at a time
In smelly underpants

Lock your house, lock your car
Buy unbreakable glass
Leave a gas can in your yard
Full of sugared gas!

I was tired of having all my stuff stolen, so I wrote a poem.

It's So Lonely Here

I let my dreams die
And I lost my heart;
Now its near the end
And I'm still at the start.

Now I sit here writing
With no future planned;
Nothing to look forward to,
I feel like I'm damned.

My life has been wasted;
I am such a fool!
If only I had started out
With some kind of clue.

It's so lonely here,
So far away from home;
With no one to believe in
And nothing but a poem.

Maybe I'll last another day,
Maybe another year;
Maybe another lifetime,
Maybe one more tear.

So I dumped it all and went truck driving; now that was hell.

Today

Today I thought I found myself
But I immediately forgot,
It's like a carrot on a stick,
Never wanting to be caught.

Today I think I lost myself
Somewhere in my mind;
Somewhere east of hearing,
Somewhere left of time.

Today I thought I lost you,
But I turned and there you were;
And although you were alone,
I'm not sure you were there.

The old insecurities...

On the Open Sea

Forever and a day
I'll sail away
To far unknown reaches,
Bright sandy beaches
And a life on the open sea.

For to make toward the isles
Where the mango man smiles;
The sun floating slowly
'Cross the skies of the holy,
Life on the open sea.

Some take to the highway,
Some take to the skyway;
Some fritter away their lives
With their children and wives
Far from the open sea.

Too soon they all die,
For life has passed by;
But I'll take my chances
With Caribbean romances
And a life on the open sea.

I'm a parrothead, I'm afraid...

Another Step

Take me to the highway
Of the future in my soul
And let me blindly go
Until I reach my goal.

Then let me die,
My journey finally done;
For I will go no further,
Whether or not I've won.

For I am so very tired,
I can hardly move;
So much effort for just on step
And another and then two.

Keep on keeping on, they say.

Depression-1997

The world is full of sorrow,
It bleeds off into space;
Only the bleak tomorrow
Looks me in the face.

I looked up from the couch
And noticed you were gone;
I changed the channel one more time
And unplugged the telephone.

As the title suggests.

The Child on the Bus

The child on the bus was eight years old,
Sensitive and mild;
He didn't speak much to the crowd
As not to get them riled.

What provoked the looks of hate,
He didn't have a clue;
But something wasn't fitting in
This pastoral view.

It wasn't race—they were all the same
As well as we all knew;
Never mentioned was religion,
I'd rule out that one, too.

Perhaps it was the easy target,
The little boy alone;
The bright pink ears like taxi doors,
Not safe till he was home.

Then his home was off the route,
Causing a detour
Of two miles per round trip
To drop him at his door.

Perhaps they heard about his brother,
Who needed special care;
To pass it on was their way
Of dealing with their fear.

A cowardly thump upon the ears
Was how it all began;
No one owning to the deed,
Again! Again! Again!

The ears are bleeding, no one heeding
The desperate pleas to stop;
The ears are bleeding, heartless teasing,
Ticking of the clock.

The taunts and teases, the little sleazes
Increase the constant pain!
The driver sees but does nothing
He's partly, then, to blame.

The ears are bleeding! No one heeding!
Driving him insane;
The ears are bleeding! Hot and heating!
Striking up a flame!

"Oh, death, come take me now, I say
Take me far away;
I couldn't really be right here,
Not here on this day!"

And consciousness is slipping fast
From the little boy
As he searches for that special place
Where all you feel is joy.

"Jerry, Alan, Brandy, Dixie
You are on my list!"
The child cries, "What kind of lies
Put them up to this?

Sandra! Sandra! What's the matter
With your shitty little life?
Goad them on, oh, harpy blonde!"
(I think she had a knife)

Ears are bleeding! No one heeding!
No one thinking twice;
Ears are bleeding! No one feeling!
Mercy! Use the knife!

And when the mob had stopped to rob
The pencils from his pack,
The bus door opened, setting free
The monster they sent back.

For as the hate would percolate
Like evil to be done,
Forty years later there's still a chance
That he could be the one.

The one to pay you back for crimes
You prob'ly don't recall;
With forty years of interest earned
That's not forgot at all.

Energy doesn't die, it's said,
It merely will transform;
And with this energy he sent a curse—
Yes, he meant them harm!

"May you never find that joy
That all of us do seek;
May you come to the very edge
And slip back from the brink!"

"Divorces, death and poverty
Shall follow all your lives;
The peace of heaven will not be yours
Nor your children, nor your wives!"

The cursing was not necessary—
The path they chose to follow
Brought them to the same results;
The lives they lived were hollow.

And passing on to wives and kids
The philosophy they felt
Will bring them to the same sad end
Lest someone prays for help.

Okay, this is a little me, a little of my friends, and a little of my brother. Actually, a lot of it is me. I decided to depict a youth of torture in one event.

The Next Drink

He sat at the bar and lit his cigar
For the first time in months, quote:
"What would it cost to just get lost
And ease this scratchy throat?"

It would cost you your wife, the love of your life
And she would take the kids;
It would cost your career you held so dear
Before you hit the skids.

It would cost you your car, you wouldn't get far—
Lose your license but you'll get
Credit for time sweating off wine
In the cell where you alit.

It would cost you the joy of watching your boy
Grow up to live your dream;
Instead he'll just drink, he has grown to think
His father and him, a team.

It will cost you the pain of the people you've slain
Behind the wheel tonight;
Haunted by ghosts, no bail you post
Will free you from their sight.

He sat at the bar, put out his cigar—
"None for me tonight!"
Picked up his wife and lived a full life,
A life that was free and right.

Dedicated to my dear little brother.

Fear

Fear is the killer,
The hunter, the deer;
The lover, the fighter
The redneck, the 'queer.'

Courage and fear
Are both the same man,
Woman and child;
Shepherd and lamb.

To understand
Is not to know
Why one is the same
And neither are both

That was from my second notebook, when I was in my 20s.

Ode to Mr. Ed

Jimmy Dean went racing
And bet upon a horse
Jimmy Dean is dead now,
But not the horse, of course

Bring back Mr. Ed
Imitations will not do
The only animal that comes close
Is Francis, the talking mule

Black and white to color
Radiation on my skin
Humor an old couch potato
Bring the horses back again.

No comment...

Archives of My Mind

Will the wind forever blow free
Chasing ripples over the sea?
Or will the waves crash upon the key
Sending her home again to me?

Will the trees forever bowing
Starve the seedling's constant growing?
Or will the sun be always glowing
Through the branches thin and folding?

But if she does not ever seed
She'll be a book for me to read,
And her fading face will be outlined
Within the archives of my mind.

I wrote this back in 1975—I enjoyed making the words bounce faster and faster, then slower and slower toward the ending.

Shades of Blue

Love in shades of blue,
Colors changing hue;
Waiting by my window,
I haven't any clue.

Blue flames of passion,
Nothing we'll ever keep;
Watching the blue horizon
Fade to the ocean deep.

In the depths of my being,
The keeper of my soul,
The color never fades
So lost, so bleak, so cold.

In the fire of existence
The image in my mind—
Off and on eternally,
Cold blue flames of time.

Another one from my early years.

Disparity

In the chilliest night
Of the coldest day
In the deepest pit
Of disparity

For the longest time
Devoid of hope,
One step at a time
Trying to cope.

Finally winning
Through surrender
I give up all
And find I never
       Had it ever.

Self-denial
Brings me all
'Fore I could stand
I had to fall.

Sometimes we must lose everything to find we had nothing; then life really begins.

Change

Can we survive the madness,
The parting of our souls;
The rending of our very beings
As we fall short of our goals?

Can we survive the terror,
The utter horror of it all?
Knowing there is nothing left
As we come against the wall?

Do we want to survive it?
Do we want to go on from here?
Or maybe it would be easier
To give in to the fear?

Can we survive the ending,,
The perfect parting of our ways;
The termination of what was,
The nighttime of our days.?

We've got a theme going here

Reflections

Reflecting on my life,
I see where I was wrong;
But I wouldn't change a thing,
I'm right where I belong.

I'm not standing still,
I'm moving fast and free;
Every day's the truth,
It changes constantly.

I never, ever lied;
When I said it, it was true.
It was part of my life
And now it's part of you.

We are small universes
Reflections of all things
And yet we are a part
Of what is reflecting.

Ode to a Rent-a-Cop

Oh, Rent-a-Cop, oh, Rent-a-Cop
With your shiny badge so bright,
Don't beat me with your nightstick;
You haven't got the right.

Your mommy must be very proud
Of her handsome little fellow;
Ironing your uniforms,
Fluffing up your pillow.

What a shame that you can't be
A real officer;
I guess that violent streak has made
You unhireable, fine sir.

But maybe there is still a chance
For a loser that is cruel;
I heard that the LAPD
Needs a man like you.

Heh, heh, heh…I used to be a security guard when I was a kid.
There were quite a few of these guys that were over the edge.

Burnside Baby

Burnside baby, gutter child;
Burnside baby, running wild;
Come to the city, come to hide;
Burnside baby, come to die.

It's always raining in the street;
The wind is cold and heartless.
Sometimes you eat, sometimes you don't;
Sometimes you stare out, thoughtless.
Darkness paints every corner,
Chimes ring out every hour;
Burnside baby, Burnside baby,
A wet and dying flower.

A shopping cart may grace your hands,
Food left in the alley;
Wine bottles carry comfort here,
Bags of rags and garbage.
Darkness paints every corner,
Chimes ring out every hour,
Burnside baby, Burnside baby,
A wet and dying flower.

Burnside Baby was a song I wrote when my little brother and I were trying to be a two-piece rock band. Burnside is a street in Portland, Oregon, where the street people tend to hang out.

Andrea

Although my daughter never calls me back
And rarely answers my frequent e-mail,
Daddy still loves his neurotic female.
Carry on, may there be nothing you lack;
To freedom, drink you deep of this fine wine
And bravely follow life where e'er it leads.
Show us mighty super-heroic deeds
That'd overshadow those which were mine;
And to tell the truth, my daughter,
Someday I'll make you proud I am your father.
All the fine items I never bought her,
All the magic of so little bother;
My precious little girl has gone away
And a young lady took her place today.

It is hard when your only daughter grows up and leaves the nest. The first few lines were only true for that short period of "breaking away."

Part Two
Death

Welcome to Chaos

The lonesome drifter came across the sign
(Perhaps it was the hour, perhaps the wine)
But as he gazed upon it, almost blind,
It read, underlined,
"Welcome to Chaos"

Confused, he fell in the wagon path
(Roll the dice and do the math).
No one screamed as it went past.
Almost dead, he said, at last,
"Welcome to Chaos."

To some the sense of his tragic end
Might escape or come again
Like a letter you might send
For the money you may spend.
Welcome to Chaos.

You might think this story is rather strange
And nothing rhymes with the color orange.
It's just your perception and your field of range;
And if your mind should ever change,
Welcome to Chaos.

Did this poem come about by my sudden grasp of the chaos theory? Or was I simply looking for an excuse to rhyme the color orange? We may never know...

The Last Christmas

In the deep frost of winter
The sun rose its head
To make its short journey
'Cross the snowy white bed;
And the garden is sleeping
Deep in the ground
Till the calling of spring
Brings it around.

And the family all gathered
For the last yearly rite
That they would all share
From morning to night;
And the presents lay silent
Under the tree,
Hiding their beauty
Till they'd be set free.

The ghosts of Christmas
Stood by for a while,
Hidden in shadows
Of blissful denial.
In mother's kitchen
The feast was prepared
And for a short while
No one was scared.

And the lilting of carols
From dust-covered tomes

Overpowered the sound
Of the sleigh going home.
When evening came 'round,
The presents unwrapped,
The children entranced,
And the parents were napped,

The stars shown so brightly
As if to say,
"Follow me home,
I'll lead the way,"
As down the old road,
Dappled in light,
One last sleigh ride
In the twinkling of night.

As the sleigh was transformed
Through heaven's thin veil,
The sun rose again
To reveal a dale;
And here it was spring
And the sleigh was a cart;
All was abloom—
For all, a new start

And here, ever after,
For those who believe,
The spirit of Christmas
Will live in a weave
Of time and dimension
Of love, death and life;
Here ever after
Through trouble and strife.

And those who survive
Year after year
Will carry the message
Of love and good cheer.
And when the last Christmas
Finally arrives
And death makes a swing
With his mighty scythe

We, too, will go
To God's promised land
And with those before
We'll walk hand in hand;
And the lonely will grieve
For the loss that they feel
Until they understand
For whom the bell peals.

The circle of life
Exists down below
But above is a globe
Of pure Christmas snow.
So happy Christmas;
Bathe in its light
And here, ever after,
To all a goodnight.

My friend and fellow poet, Richard Stalter, died shortly before Christmas in 2004, and then my stepdad passed away in February of 2005. My stepdad knew he was dying even before Thanksgiving, and I was inspired by these two men to write this poem.

The Vampire's Tale

The Vampire vanished into the night
With his cape and his cane and the red stains so bright.
A soul he has taken to refresh his own;
Another tomorrow with no going home.

High on the cliff, he screams to the sea,
"Lift off this curse you have put on to me!"
But the Witch of the Sea, with her emerald cloak,
Thinks her ex-lover as some kind of joke!

She thunders with laughter and slaps at the land
While the Vampire screams, with blood on his hands.
"Curses to you, my beloved!" she bellows,
"Curses to you, and all of your fellows!"

"Feast ye, ye shall, on all humankind,
For all of eternity in darkness and slime!"
And the Vampire walks, all alone, to his cave,
No one will try the Vampire to save.

And if you look deeply into his eyes
There is nothing but dust where tears used to hide.
And the Sea Witch rolls on, by the pull of the moon,
To find a new lover to lay in her tomb.

So if you go wandering alone in the dark;
Perhaps some night air—a stroll in the park;
And you meet an odd fellow with cold, clammy skin,
Red ruby lips and an old Scottish grin;

And you see that he hungers with needs that won't stop
And all you can hear is the tick of the clock;
Run for your life and cherish your cross;
If you have holy water, this you must toss.

Be ready with stake to cave in his skin
Where once was his heart and shall be again;
For the Vampire must die and die once again
To lift off the curse the Sea Witch did spin.

But remember, my friend, to take pity on he—
For the Vampire is slave to the Witch of the Sea.

A sudden inspiration while I was online with my old poetry group; a quick run through the many and mixed emotions of a jilted lover and the woman who took all and gave nothing.

Death

Death came to town the other day
To see what was to see,
But all there were before him
Were dying and diseased.

He touched them all, one by one,
And tried to set them free;
But he only spread before him
A world of misery.

Grieving widows,
Grieving parents,
Grieving sons and daughters;
Naught could he do to end their pain
As he touched their wives and brothers.

A missionary in his own way,
He spreads his own religion;
But for every one he tries to help
A hundred more are smitten.

But on he goes with both eyes closed
And a rattle in his pocket;
One hand in light, one in dark,
And a finger in the socket.

If there were a being called Death, then what would be his motivation?

Dream Flight

I once thought that I could fly
Over the water and through the sky
Late at night, when the color blue
Faded into misty hues;
And the wind felt soft and sang sweet songs,
And I looked down as I sailed along.

I would dream of running through the air
And leaping up without a care;
I wouldn't come down, not right away,
I'd just drift along for hours and days.

I used to dream of flying; full-color dreams of myself looking down over the river as I swept along; sometimes I would see myself running and each step longer and higher until I was leaping a hundred yards at a time.

Different

Blackest side of night
Tearing my heart out in chunks
Red colored pavement

When I was young I once saw my girl going out with another man, which in turn inspired many a song and poem, including the above poem.

Little Gigi

Oh, the icy wind blows
Playing dirges in the branches and bows
And the grass has all died and lain down
To kiss and to become the ground.
Onward we go every day
Though our friend has gone far away
And yet she sleeps at our feet
Near the garden and by Andi's tree.

A eulogy for our first little poodle, Gigi.

The Reflection of God

The pain that you're feeling
Is drifting away
On wings of butterflies
And the dawning of day.

As the sun is reborn
On the edge of the sea
And the moon slips aside
Where no one can see;

And the horrors before you
Melt in the fog,
Fading to nothing
In the reflection of God.

I had once heard that Ayatollah meant 'The Reflection of God." What a great poem idea! I remember a great old poem mentioning the slaying of an army with a glance from God, so the reflection of God seems appropriate.

Sammy

Little Sammy,
Where have you gone?
The cat's in the tree
The bird's on the lawn

And when Andi comes home
You can circle and beg;
Kick all my things
And dance on two legs.

And although you were small
Our hearts were so blessed!
With all of our love
We put you to rest.

Our second poodle—we will miss him always

Spirit

My spirit tried to leave my body;
It kicked me in the night;
I was nearly beside myself
Putting up a fight!

My spirit tried to leave my body;
It kicked me once again
Like a shot of yellow whiskey
Seeping through my skin!

How I wanted it to leave;
But still, it had to stay
For I'd be only half a man
If my spirit went away!

This was one of my English professor's favorites back in the late 70s.

The Phantom of the West Mill

As I wandered through the ravenous horde
Concocting pulp and paperboard;
The engines rumbled strong and proud,
Emitting a devilish purple shroud
As the sun set upon the West Mill.

Through the darkness, deep and dirty,
I wandered along, twenty or thirty
Minutes passed, my thinking murky,
When I caught a glimpse of shimmering light
Glowing from the bowels of the West Mill.

Dashing, dancing paper fibers
Became ghostly, misty riders
Led by one who had no face
And colorless skin; he had no race
And collected no grime from the West Mill.

The figures rode along the maze;
They faded in, then out of phase
Over the pipes, through the cutters
They stopped beside a hydropulper
And rested awhile, inside the West Mill.

Stumbling, mumbling, I pushed nearer
Bravely trying to hide my terror
But the faceless men only stared,
And, in spite of the fact that I was scared,
I approached the Phantom of the West Mill.

"Phantom, tell me, why you have come riding?
Why, now, have you come out of hiding?
Your clothing is from a bygone day;
What is it you have come to say;
And why do you travel through the West Mill?"

And as I looked into the Phantom's eyes,
I was carried away to paradise;
Beautiful people enjoying their lives;
Mothers and fathers, husbands and wives,
Unassociated with the West Mill.

So confused and lost was I
That I forgot, and that was why
I shook the hand of Wallenberg
And dropped through the floor, not even a word
Passed my lips as I fell to the West Mill.

Looking up, I saw the hole I left,
When I fell from grace and the grip of death;
I was alone by the hydropulper
And the hole closed up, complete and utter
Was my disbelief inside the West Mill.

I sat up to see if I was alone;
I called my wife but she wasn't home;
I ran outside and I looked around,
But no sign of the Phantom could be found
And there was no one else in the West Mill.

And as the lumber industry shut down
More and more phantoms could be found;
The rich got richer and the poor just died,
The unemployment rate multiplied
And crushed out the glory of the West Mill.

I have worked on this poem off and on for over 28 years. I was working as a security guard at the Longview Fibre Mill in Longview, Washington. I was on foot patrol at night, walking through the hydropulpers in a section they called the West Mill, and feeling very alone. The timber industry was on the skids and many people were unemployed, causing a general slump in the local economy. To this day the area economy is poor.

Ghosts of Little Mice

I see the ghosts of little mice
Run across the floor
Darting out from every corner
Blocking my front door

How they wiggled in my little traps
As they struggled for their freedom
The glue held them down till I came around
The mechanical traps just killed them

Frightened, they pulled and pulled
And feared a dreadful end
Starving in the garbage can
Where the trap was disposed with them

And now their ghosts won't let me be
They follow me everywhere
Every time I look around
They flee into shadow air

I can't eat, I can't sleep, I cannot work
As they weave their psychic web
I feel them running up my legs
And crawling in my bed.

True story!

The Empire

Little Caesar, can you say
How many lives you took today?
Sending his people off to war;
What do you think an army's for?
Lying to himself and fooling those
Who better knowing, would oppose
As Caesar watched with perverted joy
"How many lives can I destroy?"
He boils oil in human blood,
His country is torn with fire and flood
And his people die with no healthcare,
Demanding money that isn't there.
The oil-based smoke paints a blood-red moon—
The end of days will be here soon!
And much like Rome and old Pompeii
Falls the empire of the USA.

I gave this one the rhythm of a 60's war protest.

3 a.m. Sonnet

I wake up every night at 3 a.m.
For no apparent reason that I see
I think an inner voice is calling me
Like a salmon swimming over a dam
I know that I should try to understand
Why this happens to me every night
No longer does it give to me a fright
It is as natural as my right hand
Someday this mystery will be explained
I don't think that I am the only one
Many different reasons can be blamed
Imagining what they are can be fun
I think perhaps the dead do walk this hour
And wake me with the presence of their power.

My friend Reza and I were discussing this—we both have a tendency to suddenly wake up at 3 a.m.

The Werewolf

Oh, Mother dear, what's that I hear
Out in the woods tonight?
It sounds like pain flying through the rain
And howling with all its might

The wolves appear and run in fear
Of the devil-beast afar
Covered with hair and blood-soaked where
His prey was torn apart

Oh, Mother dear, will he come here?
Are we safe at home this time?
For the wind it blows
And the river flows
Above the water line

Calm yourself and do not fret
So much my little child
We are high above and across the flood
From where the man-beast hides

But he could swim; could not he, then,
Entrap us on this hill?
I've seen our dog (where is our dog?)
Paddle where he will

Think not, my child, of such things
For they will help you not
It senses fear, and it brings him here
Control your fearful thoughts!

Oh, Mother dear, I can't but fear
What is scratching at our door?
I fear he's come to take your own
Away for evermore!

I'm sure it's just the dog come back
From wherever he had roamed
He's back to keep us safe tonight
To be fed and bathed and combed

I think we, then, should let him in
Where it's safe and dry
To leave him lie where the man-beast cries
Is to condemn our friend to die

Oh, the love of man for his pets
Comes close to godliness
But to open that door while the moon is full
Would be pure foolishness

When the sun returned the following day
And the weather again was mild
The faithful pet did mourn the loss
Of the mother and her child.

A werewolf? Or a child abuser?

Part Three
Love

Friends

My friend you are and always shall it be
No one can take away our inner peace
Soon, way too soon, it seems, our lives will cease
Then once again our souls, they will be free
My role as an accountant will expire
Her youth and all her glory will soon fade
Never spinning the wheel that I made
Always picking yourself out of the fire
If summers could be put into a shell
And winters cold could be warmed by a thought
And angels from the heavens never fell
And if leprechauns ever could be caught
Then one day when our souls are off in flight
Our consciousness may finally touch the light.

As I recall, I was bouncing poems back and forth in a "friendly" online competition with a lady poet that went by Moonlupis; so I embedded her "handle" in a sonnet.

Immortal Beloved

Immortal beloved, where are you now?
Have you no voice with which to speak to me?
Have I not the ears with which to hear thee?
Will we never make a true lovers' vow?
Immortal beloved, I am alone.
I stand here amazed at my solitude.
Perhaps it is my melancholy mood;
Nothing but silence comes from my phone.
I look for your letter every day
Or perhaps a sign in the tarot cards.
I'll cast my body out into the bay
And break into a thousand brittle shards
And as the pieces turn to gentle sand
She'll pick me up and run me through her hand.

I saw a great movie about Beethoven called Immortal Beloved *and I just had to have a poem of the same name. To reference the immortal part, I mention tarot cards and telephones— something old and something new to symbolize immortality.*

2022

In the twilight of my life
Will you still be there?
Is this thing forever?
Do you really care?

When I'm old and ugly,
Children run in fear,
Will you be there to comfort me,
And dry away the tear?

Is this thing forever?
Are you needing too?
Will we hold each other
In 2022?

Will we forgive transgressions
As we stumble through our lives?
Keeping sacred the holy trust
Welling in our eyes?

At the very least we're partners,
At the very most we're God
But for now we're somewhere in between,
The even and the odd.

Just pondering the future...

Seven Keys

Just as if she had been here all along,
Near to my heart, the aching I can feel.
Can we be when on one knee I kneel,
When all night long I yearn to hear her song?
Then if jet planes fly above the city;
Then if dreams come true for me and for you;
Then if ever I've acted like a fool;
Then if a river flows to a jetty,
Then ever my fallen angel shall be
Safely in my vision of the heavens;
Protected always by a simple key,
For the children once knew the rule of seven:
For thrice the vision counted out a sign
And thrice the very soul of love was mine.

This is that poetry exchange mentioned earlier; I think Jennifer was Moonlupis' real name. By the way, the seventh key is the name embedded in the sonnet.

Insomnia

I lie awake and think of you;
Of what you say and what you do;
Of who we are and what must be;
Of why you said what you said to me.

I see your face in a distant place;
In an airport we make a fond embrace.
When I close my eyes and concentrate
We kiss and touch and melt and mate.

Our passion burns all through the night
Then I take you back to catch your flight.
Maybe we'll never meet again—
And suddenly it's six a.m.

Have you ever had one of those dreams where you thought you were daydreaming and suddenly it was morning?

I Look for Love

Quietly the sun gives to the moon.
Softly her footsteps cross the room.
But even as the moonlight
Is reflecting off her hair,
I realize that something isn't there.

Where is the woman that wandered through my life;
The woman that I had asked someday to be my wife?
Have the days and nights been all that unfair?
I look for love and find it isn't there.

Are foolish dreams the reason for my fall?
If it weren't for her, I'd have no dreams at all.
And now she has no words to say as I lay in despair;
She gave me love, and now it isn't there.

Silently she turns her head to sleep.
Quietly toward the door I creep.
In the morning when she wakes up and finds that I'm not there
She'll look for love and find it isn't there.

I was working as a security guard back in 1977. The only station that would come in was a country station that drifted in from the other side of Washington state. Suddenly, in the middle of the night, I stopped the patrol truck and wrote two songs, as fast as my hand could move. This is one of them.

Forever

Is love so special
That only two may share
Or could there be enough in one
For another one to share?

Is love forever
Or does it fade away;
Metamorphasizing
To what, I cannot say?

Is love today,
Tomorrow, or next year;
Or yesterday, hereafter,
Never more to share?

Can I live without you,
Can I live alone;
Can I live at all,
Forever, all alone?

Ah! My insecurities getting the better of me!

Love Me Forever

Love me forever!
Elate me with your touch;
Bring me ever higher,
I've never loved so much!

Float me down the river
Of love's sweet flowing grace;
Drown me in your water,
Locked in our embrace.

Love whome'er you feel
All your many days;
But as you spin the wheel,
Don't forget my face.

I can't help it; sometimes I am just overcome with love! And then insecurity slips in...

The Cold, Cold Sun

The circle came full 'round
To the cold side of the light;
There we were in darkness,
Warmed by our delight.
Time passing much to quickly,
Much too fast to keep;
The cold, cold sun rose completely
And froze us in our sleep.
And as we stood in solitude,
Each one like a stone,
I thought to myself, "How could such light
Leave us cold and all alone?"
And as I pondered my situation
The sun began to fade
And I began to seek for warmth
Deeper in the shade;
And when I got there, there you were—
Back from day's long run;
And as we touched the heat returned,
Free from the cold, cold sun.

I posted this online once; as far as I could tell, no one understood it. You need to follow the feeling, guided by the words; for most of us, the evening is when you are with your beloved, heated by your love and affection; but by day you must be apart, earning livings and dealing with the world. The heat of love only returns at night when you can be together again.

In a Kiss

You are my first thought in the morning,
You are my first dream in the night;
Just your touch can make my day,
Just your smile can give me life.

When I feel like letting go
And giving up my place,
Your face lights up my shadowed mind
And lifts me into grace.

And your voice floats on the evening breeze,
And soothes my troubled heart;
And your smile, when you look at me,
Breaks the night apart.

And in my mind we will always be
Together for all time;
Even though I may never find
A way to make you mine.

Just know that I love you
And it will be have to do;
You are my soul split off from me
Yet still here in me, too

And some day when all is known
And we return to the mist,
the energy that once was us
Will mingle in a kiss.

My insecurities again—does my wife really love me?

Love Is a Diamond

Love is a diamond—
Cold, hard and blue;
The buyers are many,
The keepers are few.

A diamond is love—
Costly and dear;
Spiritually cloudy,
Physically clear.

Love is the climate
And diamonds, the dust
That gets in your eyes
When the climate's unjust.

One of my earliest works.

For You

If there were some way I could say
Well, not really anyway
If there were something I could do
I'd do it for you

If there were someone I could trust
It'd be you I know that it must
I hope that my feelings are just
And won't offend you

And it just goes to show
How much that I know
And if I hurt you someway
I'm sorry I say

That I want to hold you so much
I just need somebody to touch
I hope I'm not asking too much
But here I go

If there were some way I could say
Well, not really anyway
If there were something I could do
I'd do it for you.

I write because when I speak, it comes out this way.

Union Station

Sometimes late at night when I'm feeling kinda low
I take myself out, I don't know where I go
I'm looking for you, baby, trying to find a sign
It seems to me lately you're always on my mind

You can shout it out from the Union Station
But you won't find a man in this whole nation
Who'll love you as much as the way that I do
I've got a dollar in my sock and a hole in my shoe
I miss you.

You can laugh in my face, you think you're pretty funny
I've given you, baby, all of my money
I've given you everything I've got in the world
My friends say I should find another girl

You can shout it out from the Union Station
But you won't find a man in this whole nation
Who'll love you as much as the way that I do
I've got a dollar in my sock and a hole in my shoe
I miss you.

Sometimes late at night I take myself out
And I wander around, then I turn and I shout
"My God! I wish you were here with me
Been crying so much I can hardly see!"

You can shout it out from the Union Station
But you won't find a man in this whole nation
Who'll love you as much as the way that I do
I've got a dollar in my sock and a hole in my shoe
I miss you.

A song I wrote in 1999.

Grace

For years I had been searching
But I never thought I'd find
A love so overwhelming
Lasting for all time

Through the darkness, struggling,
Looking for my place
And you gave to me your hand
And shared with me your grace.

My thankfulness for finding love.

1975

I remember walking away
Crying without shame
I saw you there with him
And all was lost again

How could I have been so desperate
To seek forever in your eyes?
When I gave you my wholeness
You showered me with lies.

That incident when I was young, still producing art.

A Moment

I see the morning in your eyes
The joy of completion
As one we must exist
Parted for too long
Your heart beats in my ears
Your breath fills my lungs
Your existence gives me life

Your beauty pulls at my soul
A statue in a garden
A flower in a meadow
A light in the storm
And if we never meet again
I can say that I touched heaven
Just for a moment.

I honestly can't remember writing this.

Shades of the Heart

There was a man in Phoenix
With a story to tell;
How he kept trying for heaven
And found himself in hell.

I don't know if he loved her,
I guess I'll never know;
From the depth of how he held her
You would think he'd never go.

But there he was days later,
Another in his arms;
The passion flowing through him
No matter who he harms.

He didn't know that she
Had lovers on the side;
He thought he had her wrapped
Up and she would never lie.

And would they be surprised
If one day they both found
That when they had it all
They had nothing but the sound

Of two hearts beating silent,
Far from love's sharp ears;
Shades of the heart unveiled,
Bathed in salted tears.

I was listening to a song that I think was called "Shape of My Heart," and I was thinking that didn't make sense and pondered what would make sense—I came up with "Shades of the Heart."

Pamela

Perhaps her life was not the way she planned
Far from the path on which she built her dream
Come rainy day, come sunshine's radiant beam
Come back to me whose feet are made of sand
Everlasting love may yet be mine
Everlasting peace is her desire
Flying jump from the pan into the fire
And only enter when she sees the sign
Forever all I do, I do for her
Forever all she sees is what I've done
Forever all is lost in what we were
Forever all too much and there was none
To take us to sit at Eros' right arm
And live our fitting lives so free from harm.

A sonnet with an embedded name—one of my favorite tricks.